WHAT Will HATCH?

JENNIFER WARD

illustrated by **SUSIE GHAHREMANI**

WALKER BOOKS FOR YOUNG READERS
AN IMPRINT OF BLOOMSBURY
NEW YORK   LONDON   NEW DELHI   SYDNEY

SANDY
ball.

WHAT will HATCH?

PADDLE
and
CRAWL—

SEA TURTLE.

WARM seat.

WHAT
will
HATCH?

ON DADDY's feet—

PENGUIN.

JELLY,
jiggly.

WHAT
will
HATCH?

WIGGLY, squiggly —

WHAT will HATCH?

TOOTHY
smile—

CROCODILE.

ROBIN.

YELLOW,
tiny.

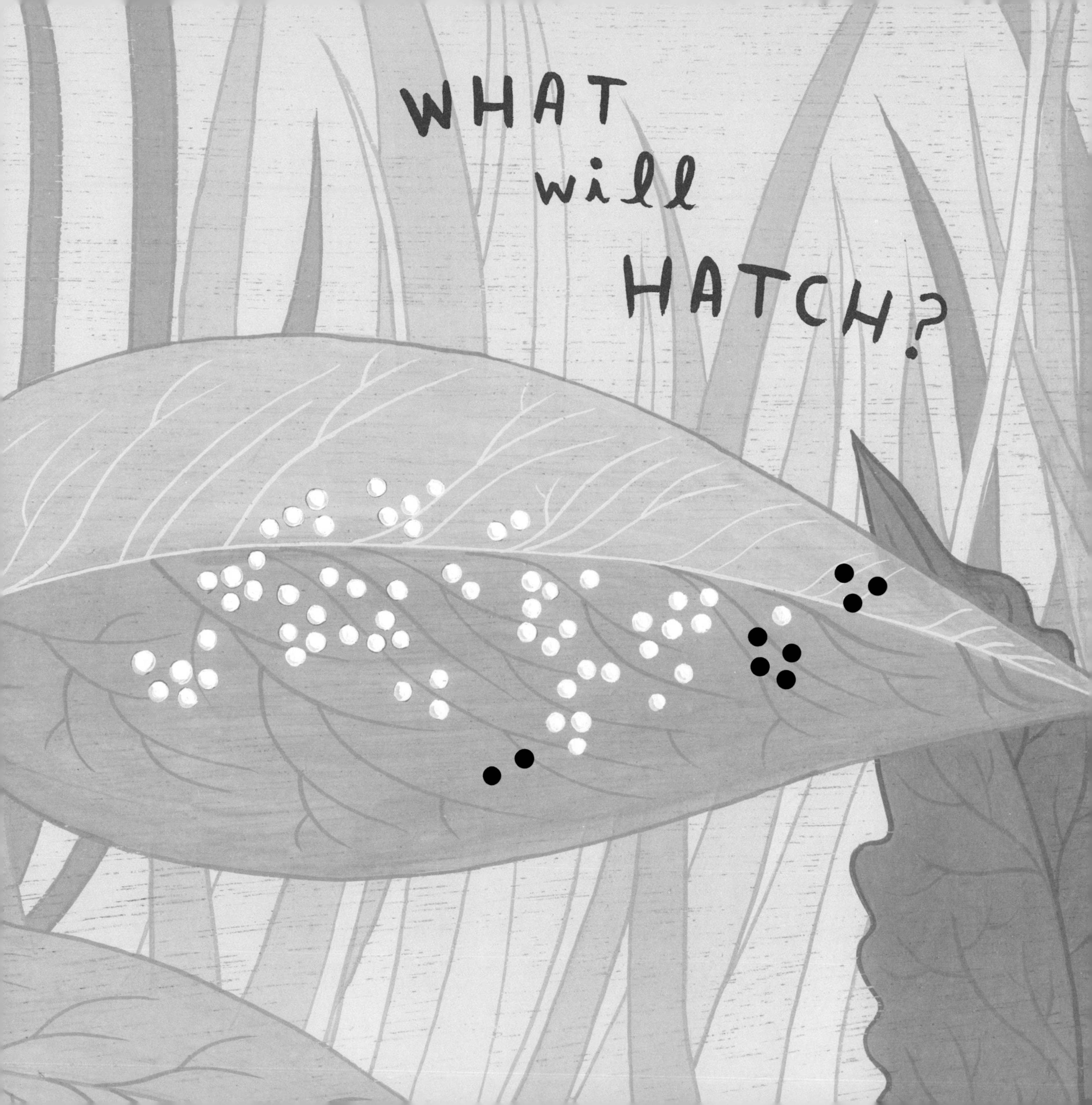
WHAT
will
HATCH?

CATERPILLAR.

SMALL,
leathery.

WHAT will HATCH?

PLATYPUS!

OVIPAROUS ANIMALS...

Oviparous animals hatch from eggs. Oviparous animals include all birds, most insects, amphibians, reptiles, fish, and just two types of mammals—the echidna and the platypus.

CATERPILLAR

TIME IN EGG: Ten days to two weeks, depending on species

MOTHER: Lays eggs, then leaves

WHERE: On a host plant that the caterpillar will eat after hatching

SIBLINGS: Hundreds

GOLDFINCH

(cover bird)

TIME IN EGG: Twelve to fourteen days

MOTHER: Lays and incubates eggs; father feeds chicks after they hatch

WHERE: A cup-shaped nest in a tree or shrub

SIBLINGS: Two to seven

CROCODILE

TIME IN EGG: Around two to three months

MOTHER: Guards eggs and protects babies after they hatch

WHERE: A nest in the soil (dirt or sand)

SIBLINGS: Twenty to sixty, depending on species

PENGUIN

TIME IN EGG: About sixty-four days for the emperor penguin

MOTHER: Father incubates egg

WHERE: On top of the father's feet, under a layer of skin and feathers called a "brood pouch"

SIBLINGS: None

ROBIN

TIME IN EGG: About fourteen days

MOTHER: Incubates eggs; both mother and father care for young after they hatch

WHERE: A cup-shaped nest in a tree or shrub

SIBLINGS: Two to four per clutch

PLATYPUS

TIME IN EGG: About ten days

MOTHER: Incubates eggs and cares for young after they are born

WHERE: In a burrow

SIBLINGS: One or two

SEA TURTLE

TIME IN EGG: About sixty days, depending on species

MOTHER: Lays eggs and heads back to sea

WHERE: Sandy nest dug on shoreline

SIBLINGS: About forty-nine to 199, depending on species

TADPOLE

TIME IN EGG: About six to twenty-one days, depending on species

MOTHER: Most frog moms leave the eggs after laying them

WHERE: In water or wet places on land

SIBLINGS: About one thousand to two thousand eggs laid, but only a few will survive to become frogs

CHICKEN EGG DEVELOPMENT

DAY 1: embryo

DAY 7: embryo

DAY 14: embryo

DAY 21: NEW CHICK!

CHICKEN

TIME IN EGG: About twenty-one days

MOTHER: Incubates eggs and cares for young after they hatch

WHERE: In a nesting box or in a shallow nest on the ground

SIBLINGS: Varies from clutch to clutch, but usually seven to eleven